50 Mistakes Grant Writers Make
Easy to Use Tips For Writing Winning Grant Proposals

by
Vanessa Collins

Heart Thoughts Publishing
Floyds Knobs, IN

HEART THOUGHTS PUBLISHING

50 Mistakes Grant Writers Make
Copyright © 2013 by Vanessa Collins

Request for information should be addressed to:
Heart Thoughts Publishing, P.O. Box 536, Floyds Knobs, IN 47119

All rights reserved. This book or any portion thereof may not be reproduced or used in any manner whatsoever without the express written permission of the publisher except for the use of brief quotations in a book review.

Cover Design: Vanessa Collins
Editor: Janice McCauly

ISBN 1494342308

Heart Thoughts Publishing
P.O. Box 536
Floyds Knobs, IN 47119
www.HeartThoughtsPublishing.com
Vanessa@HeartThoughtsPublishing.com

Printed in the United States of America

First Printing, 2013

Table of Contents

Introduction 6
Mistake #1 – Poor Writing 9
Mistake #2 – Grammar Errors 10
Mistake #3 – Spelling Errors 16
Mistake #4 – Punctuation Errors 18
Mistake #5 – Not Following Instructions 22
Mistake #6 – Submitting a Proposal Late 23
Mistake #7 – Does Not Follow Page Formatting Guidelines 23
Mistake #8 – All Required Attachments and Information Not Included 24
Mistake #9 – Organization Has Not Been Formally Incorporated 24
Mistake #10 – Legal Name Does Not Match DUN Number Registration 25
Mistake #11 – Organization Does Not Have or Did Not Include EIN ... 25
Mistake #12 – Did Not Include Congressional District (if applicable) .. 26
Mistake #13 – Did Not Include Proof of IRS Tax Exempt Status (if applicable) 26
Mistake #14 – Project Title Missing or Vague 27
Mistake #15 – Abstract is Not Included or Poorly Written 27
Mistake #16 – The Problem Addressed in the Proposal is Not Significant 28
Mistake #17 – Proposal Does Not Include Enough Documentation about the Problem 29
Mistake #18 – Proposal Does Not Specifically State How the Money will be Used 29
Mistake #19 – Proposal Does Not Demonstrate Creativity or Innovation 30

Mistake #20 – Literature Review Does Not Include Relevant Research 30

Mistake #21 – Needs Assessment Does Not Clearly Articulate the Project Audience and Its Needs 32

Mistake #22 – Does Not Provide Evidence That Project Activities and Goals Directly Address the Needs of the Identified Audience 32

Mistake #23 – Does Not Clearly State Project Goals and Objectives ... 33

Mistake #24 – Does Not Clearly State the Design, Integration, and Implementation of an Evaluation Method that will Measure Project Results 35

Mistake #25 – Does Not Include Information About the Roles and Commitments of Partnering Organizations, if applicable 35

Mistake #26 – Does Not Identify Key Project Staff, Their Duties, and Their Qualifications for Successfully Completing Their Project Tasks .. 36

Mistake #27 – Does Not Identify Consultants and Service Providers Involved in Project Activities, the Process for Selecting Them, and How They Will Work With Project Staff 37

Mistake #28 – Does Not Include a Timeline for Specific Activities 37

Mistake #29 – Does Not Describe the Facilities, Equipment, and Supplies Necessary to Support the Project 38

Mistake #30 – Does Not Identify Source(s) of Matching Funds and/or In-kind Contributions (if applicable) 38

Mistake #31 – Does Not Identify Source(s) and Use of Revenues That Will be Derived From the Project, if applicable 39

Mistake #32 – Does Not Reflect Evidence of Sound Financial Management Coupled with an Appropriate and Cost-efficient Budget. 39

Mistake #33 – Does Not Reflect Evidence That All Partners are Active Contributors to the Partnership Activities (if applicable) 40

Mistake #34 – Evidence That the Project's Benefits Can be Sustained Beyond the Grant Period 40

Mistake #35 – Proposal Includes Not Enough Detail or Too Much Detail 40

Mistake #36 – Proposal is Not Drawing a Clear Link Between Need, Plan, and Budget 41

Mistake #37 – Proposal Sloppy and Difficult to Read 41

Mistake #38 – Proposal Filled with Jargon 42

Mistake #39 – Organization Does Not Document Success with Other Grants/Projects 42

Mistake #40 – Organization Does Not Demonstrate Financial Stability 43

Mistake #41 – The Project Doesn't Match the Funder's Objectives or Areas of Interest 43

Mistake #42 – Budget is Incomplete 43

Mistake #43 – Budget Contains Math Errors 44

Mistake #44 – Projected Income/Resources Do Not Make Sense 44

Mistake #45 – Projected Expenses Do Not Make Sense 44

Mistake #46 – Budget Narrative Does Not Justify Amounts 45

Mistake #47 – Budget Numbers Do Not Match Narrative and/or Summary 45

Mistake #48 – Required financial records are not included 45

Mistake #49 – Company Balance Sheet is Incorrect or Out of Balance 46

Mistake #50 – Company Previous Profit/Loss Statements are Incorrect 46

References 47

Introduction

"The need is so great and the work is so important."

This is the reason why most non-profit agencies believe that their project should be funded. Their program is addressing a problem that is so big in the community that anyone who has "half a brain" would jump at the opportunity to help. Or so they think. They submit their proposal, only to receive a letter stating that their proposal has not been chosen.

There are many reasons why grant proposals are not chosen. Sometimes it is simply the fact that a limited amount of money has been allocated for that funding cycle. That is something, as a grant writer, you cannot control. However, many times grant proposals are not funded because the proposal itself was poorly written. The ideas were not clear or there was a glaring error in the budget. Maybe a section was completed incorrectly or missing entirely. As a result, the proposal was rejected due to a process of elimination.

You may not be able to control how much money is available for a particular grant program or how many proposals are competing for those resources. However, you can control how your proposal looks and how clearly the ideas are presented.

The purpose of this book is to help you, the grant writer, present your case in the best way possible. Although there are many errors that can be made when preparing a grant proposal, we have chosen 50 of the most common mistakes grant writers make to highlight here. The information presented here, including the checklist available on our website, will make it easy for you to evaluate your proposal before you submit it.

If you are a professional grant writer who writes and submits a number of grant proposals every year, these mistakes may seem trivial. However, if you do not write grant proposals on a regular basis and grant writing is one of the many hats that you wear in your organization, this book was designed for you.

Why I Wrote This Book

My inspiration for this book comes out of a very similar situation. As the administrator and head teacher for a Christian daycare center and school in Northwest Indiana, I wore many hats, including grant writer. Our program had about 200 children, ranging from 6 weeks to 16 years old. On any given day I would have to teach my class (girls 5th – 9th grade), prepare and coordinate curriculum for grades 1st thru 10th, speak with parents, assist other teachers, attend meetings and maybe even help in the cafeteria. If I happened to find a grant opportunity that our program would benefit from, it was up to me, as school administrator, to seek it out and prepare the grant proposal for submission.

Finding someone to review my proposals before submission was always a little tricky. While the principal and other people that I could convince to quickly read over my proposal would point out a few typos, they really did not have the time to read the Request for Proposal and my draft submission to make sure that I was addressing everything that was required. They simply did not know exactly what to look for. Having a tool, like the one presented here, would have made that process a lot easier.

How to Use This Book

This book actually contains two parts. Part One list each of the 50 mistakes with a brief explanation of what it is and tips on how to correct it. Part Two is a checklist that lists each of the mistakes in a concise format that can be used when evaluating your grant proposals. You can download the checklist from our website . Feel free to copy the checklist as long as you keep the credit and copyright information intact.

We know that this book will make your grant writing task a little easier. If you find that it was helpful, please leave a favorable rating on Amazon. If you would like someone to review your grant proposal using this same criteria, please contact visit our website www.VanessaCollinsLLC.com. Our editors would love to assist you.

Mistake #1 – Poor Writing

Many proposals are tossed to the side after the grant reviewer reads the first page. If your proposal is poorly written, it could be eliminated immediately. Grant reviewers are reading a number of proposals at a time, many with similar needs and project audiences. What will make your proposal stick out from all of the rest? Your proposal is literally fighting for the attention of the reviewer in the midst of the stack of other proposals screaming for that same attention. Poor writing will shut your proposal down immediately.

No matter how great you think you are at writing, you must have your proposal proofread by someone who is a better writer than yourself. Find a retired teacher or a college student that is majoring in English and pay them to proofread your proposal. It is a known fact: YOU CANNOT EDIT YOUR OWN WORK.

Your proposal should be clear and concise. Have someone who is not familiar with your mission read your proposal for clarity. Avoid using big words just for the sake of using big words. Make sure that your proposal tells a compelling story without being overly sentimental. Avoid overusing jargon and buzzwords. Make sure that you spell out acronyms the first time you use them. Do not assume that the reviewer knows what you are talking about. Try to avoid long paragraphs if possible.

Following is a checklist that you can use when evaluating how well your proposal is written.

- Are complete sentences used, meaning that each sentence has a subject and predicate?
- Do all sentences begin with a capital letter?

- Do all proper nouns begin with capital letters?
- Are periods and commas used correctly?
- Are quotations punctuated correctly?
- Are apostrophes used correctly?
- Do all main verbs agree with the subject in person and number?
- Are any parts of verb phrases missing or incorrect?
- Are verb endings correct?
- Is the verb tense correct?
- Are helping verbs used when needed?
- Do regular plurals end in "s"?
- Are irregular plurals correct?
- Are articles "a", "an", and "the" used correctly?
- Does every pronoun have a clear referent?
- Are words spelled correctly? (Be careful of words that sound the same but have different meanings.)
- Are words used that give a picture of what is taking place?
- Are transitional words used?
- Do sentences begin with different words?
- Did the writer use a variety of words in each sentence?

Mistake #2 – Grammar Errors

Although the overall quality of the grant proposal was discussed in Mistake #1, we will look at specific writing errors in the next few sections.

Grammar is the set of rules which govern how words are put together to form sentences. These rules include what words are used in a particular situation. In the English language, this can be complicated by the fact that we have different words that have similar meanings such as the words "large" and "big"; words that sound the same but have very different meanings such as "there" and "their"; and words that are spelled the same but have different meanings and pronunciations, depending on how they are used in the sentence. An example is close, which is pronounced CLOZE if the meaning is "to shut" or CLOS if the meaning is "near." Another complication is that many people write the way they speak, and most people to do not always follow the proper grammatical rules they were taught in school when they speak.

Below is a list common grammar rules that you should keep in mind when preparing your proposal.

Accept/Except

"Accept" is a verb meaning to receive, to hold as true or to answer yes. "Except" is most often used as a preposition meaning apart from or excluding.

Correct: *The office will accept applications before 10:00 AM.*

Correct: *I love those cars except the blue one.*

Attain/Obtain

Both "attain" and "obtain" mean to gain or achieve something. However, "attain" implies that there is an amount of work or difficulty needed for acquisition. It also speaks to reaching a certain state or condition. "Obtain" means "to get" and is generally used to denote the possession of an object.

Correct: *Students in our program attain a level of success greater than those who do not participate.*

Correct *I must obtain three letters of recommendation before I submit my application.*

Farther/Further

Use the word "farther" if you are speaking of a measurable distance. "Further should be used if you speaking of an abstract or figurative distance.

Correct: *We must drive farther to reach the community center.*

Correct: *The further in debt we are, the worse it will be for our organization.*

Fewer/Less

Use "fewer" with things you can count. Use "less" with collective nouns, things that you may not count individually.

Correct: *We received fewer applications this year than last.*

Correct: *There is less funding available this year for educational programs.*

Collective nouns can be identified by the fact that we generally do not make them plural. We would not make the word "funding" plural. Therefore, it is a collective noun.

i.e./e.g.

Use "i.e." when you are going to further explain a comment you have just made. It is typically used within parentheses with a comma immediately follow it.

Correct: *Faith-based organizations (i.e., those that have mission statements based on religious principles) will not be able to apply.*

Use "e.g." when you are going to provide one or more examples of something you have just said. It is typically used within parentheses with a comma immediately follow it.

Correct: *Faith-based organizations (e.g., churches, synagogues or mosques) will not be able to apply.*

May/Might

Use the word "may" if there is a possibility of the outcome happening. Use the word "might" if the outcome is less likely or uncertain.

Correct: *We may purchase computers from several vendors on the preferred vendor's list. (The outcome is likely.)*

Correct: *We might build a facility on Mars someday. (The outcome is less likely.)*

There is an exception. "Might" is the past tense for the word "may". So use "might" for everything referring to the past, even if the outcome was likely.

Incorrect: *He may have applied for this grant before.*

Correct: *He might have applied for this grant before.*

The other exception is if you are writing about something not happening. Since the word "may" also means "having permission", it can be confusing if you use the phrase "may not".

Incorrect: *The vendor may not attend the function. (Is the vendor not going because they refuse to go or are forbidden to go?)*

Correct: *The vendor might not attend the function.*

Since/Because

Many teachers believe that "since" and "because" can be used interchangeably. However, it can be a little confusing. "Since" refers to time and "because" refers to causation.

Correct: *Since we published our newsletter, we have received several phone calls. (This refers to a span of time.)*

Correct: *Because we included an ad for our new books, sales have increases 10%. (This reflects a cause/effect relationship).*

That/Which

"That" is a pronoun used in a restrictive clause. A restrictive clause is a part of the sentence that is specific to the noun that it is referring to. Removing this clause will change the meaning of the sentence.

Correct: *Applications that are for minors require a parent's signature.*

The phrase "that are for minors" restricts the types of applications that are being referred to. If you remove the phrase, you are left with a sentence that has a different meaning. Restrictive clauses do not have commas separating it from the sentence.

"Which" is used in nonrestrictive clauses. Nonrestrictive clauses do not change the meaning of the sentence. They just add additional information.

Correct: *The applications, which are found at the Post Office, must be filled out with black ink.*

The phrase "which are found at the Post Office" can be removed without changing the meaning of the sentence. Nonrestrictive clauses are separated from the rest of the sentence by commas.

That/Who

Use the word "who" whenever you are referring to people.

Incorrect: *Mr. Smith is the person that will lead our fundraising efforts.*

Correct: *Mr. Smith is the person who will lead our fundraising efforts.*

Whether/If

Use the word "whether" if there are two or more choices. Use "if" if there are no alternatives.

Correct: *She did not know whether the proposal was due Monday or Tuesday.*

Correct: *She can apply for the loan if she has the correct information.*

Using "if" or "whether" also depends on whether the statement is conditional or not. Use "if" if the statement is conditional. Use "whether" if the statement is not conditional.

Correct: *Call the office if you are going to be late. (You are only expected to call if you are going to be late).*

Correct: *Call the office whether or not you receive the package on Monday. (You are expected to call either way).*

Whether/Whether or Not

The phrase "whether or not" should only be used if you mean "regardless of whether" as in the last example in the previous section. If adding "or not" does not change the meaning of the sentence, leave it off.

Incorrect: *She did not know whether or not to submit the proposal Monday or Tuesday.*

Correct: *She did not know whether to submit the proposal on Monday or Tuesday.*

Who/Whom

The word "who" is a pronoun that is used as the subject of a clause. It is similar to the words "he", "she", "it", "we", and "they". The word "whom" is pronoun that acts as the object of a clause. It is similar to "him", "her", "it", "us", and "them". Determine whether you are referring to the subject or the object of the clause. A quick way to figure out which word to use is to substitute "who" or "whom" with "he" or "him" and see which one sounds correct.

Correct: *Who is taking care of the financial report?* He is taking care of the financial report. "Him is taking care of the financial report" would be incorrect.

Correct: *I contacted an accountant whom I worked with before.* I contacted him. "I contacted he" would be incorrect.

Mistake #3 – Spelling Errors

All word processing programs these days are equipped with a spell checker. However, even spell check can miss words from time to time especially if the word is misused. Following is a list of commonly misspelled words.

acceptable	fiery
accidentally	foreign
accommodate	fourth
acquire	gauge
acquit	generally
a lot	grammar
amateur	grateful
apparent	guarantee
argument	harass
atheist	height
believe	hierarchy
calendar	ignorance
category	immediate
cemetery	independent
changeable	indispensable
collectible	intelligence
committed	its / it's
conscience	knowledge
conscientious	leisure
conscious	library
definite(ly)	lightning
disappear	maintenance
discipline	manoeuvre
dollar	memento
drunkenness	millennium
embarrass	miniature
equipment	mischievous
exhilarate	noticeable
exceed	occasion
existence	occasionally
experience	occur / occurred

occurrence	rhythm
official	sandal
parallel	schedule
parliament	scissors
pastime	sensible
pigeon	separate
possession	special
preferable	success
principal / principle	to / too / two
privilege	tomorrow
questionnaire	their / they're / there
receive	twelfth
recommend	tyranny
referred	until
reference	vacuum
relevant	vicious
religious	weather
restaurant	weird
ridiculous	you're / your

Mistake #4 – Punctuation Errors

Many common punctuation errors deal with the proper use of commas, semi-colons, colons. Consider these following rules.

Comma Usage

A comma splice occurs when two complete sentences are joined by only a comma.

Incorrect: *Our teachers will provide instruction to the students, upperclassmen will serve as tutors.*

Many times it is better to simple separate the two sentences using a period.

Correct: *Our teachers will provide instruction to the students. Upperclassmen will serve as tutors.*

If you choose to link the two sentences, you must use either a semicolon or a comma with a coordinating conjunction.

Correct: *Our teachers will provide instruction to the students; upperclassmen will serve as tutors.*

Correct: *Our teachers will provide instruction to the students, and upperclassmen will serve as tutors.*

Commas in a series

If you list three or more items in a series, use a comma to separate them. For years students were taught to use a common between the second to last item in the series and the conjunction "and". In recent years, this rule has been relaxed. However, in formal writing, you may still use it.

Correct: *We are looking to purchase computers, software, and printers.*

Commas and Coordinate Adjectives

When using a number of adjectives together, use a comma to separate them, most of the time. The exception to this rule is if the modifier would not make sense with the word "and" added.

Correct: *The facility was located in an old, run-down building. (You could say that the building was old and run-down.)*

Correct: *The little old lady stood on the sidewalk. (You would not say that the lady was little and old. Therefore you would not use a comma.)*

Commas with Quoted Material

Generally, a comma is used to separate a quotation from the rest of the sentence.

Correct: *The administrator stated, "We are looking forward to visiting your facility."*

If the quoted material is in the middle of the sentence, use two commas to separate the quote.

Correct: *"I am not sure," she said, "how to proceed."*

However, you do not use commas to separate quoted materials that are proceeded by the word "that" or quoted for the purpose of emphasis.

Correct: *The administrator told us that "the purpose of the meeting was to learn about marketing".*

Correct: *We have not seen the "capital gains" that were promised by the manager.*

Commas for Contrast

Use commas to separate phrases that show contrast.

Correct: *The facility was nice, but very small.*

Semi-colons

When connecting two independent clauses without conjunctions (*and, but, for, or, nor, so, yet*) you must use a semi-colon.

Correct: *Stop by the office tonight; I will give you the package.*

When connecting two independent clauses with a conjunctive adverb (such as "however" or "therefore) or transitional phrases (such as "in addition" or "in fact") you must use a semi-colon.

Incorrect: *The organization has raised substantial money in the past, however, recent changes to the tax laws have made fundraising difficult.*

Correct: *The organization has raised substantial money in the past; however, recent changes to the tax laws have made fundraising difficult.*

Colon

Use the colon to introduce a list of items after a complete sentence.

Correct: *You will be required to bring several items: driver's license, social security card, check stubs and prove of residency.*

Use a colon two sentences when the second sentence explains the first sentence without the use of a coordinating conjunction.

Correct: *The reading facility will provide tutoring: tutors from the local college will be recruited.*

Mistake #5 – Not Following Instructions

Many great proposals lose points because the applicant did not follow the directions. Make sure that you carefully read the instructions for the grant proposal before you begin to assemble your application. Also read the instructions again after you have completed the application. You will often find things that you missed during the first reading. Make sure to read the instructions even if you have applied and received funding from a particular organization in the past. Oftentimes applications and instructions are updated without your knowledge.

Below is a list of common elements addressed in the instructions for a grant proposal. Make sure that you read the specific instructions for your proposal to see how to handle these items.

- Cover Page – Are you required to submit a cover page?

- Number of copies – How many copies are required for submission? Are there any specific instructions on how the copies should be collated (i.e., no staples, staple on upper left side, no paper clips, etc.)?

- Where to submit – Do you have the correct address for submitting the application? Do you have to submit the application online?

- When to submit – Will the application be postmarked by the required date? If you are submitting online, are you familiar with the website that you will submit your application to? **Note: You do not want to wait until 4:30 PM to log on** to a website that requires a 5:00 PM application submission.

- Have you submitted all of the required attachments? Many grants are automatically eliminated because all of the information requested was not submitted.

Mistake #6 – Submitting a Proposal Late

Most agencies will NOT accept a late proposal. Make sure you have adequately planned for situations that may arise that could prevent you from submitting your application on time. Make sure that you know for certain when an application is due. Some applications must be "postmarked by" a certain date while others must be "received by" a certain date. If you are submitting your application by mail and it has a "postmarked by" requirement, make sure you know what time your local Post Office closes.

Mistake #7 – Does Not Follow Page Formatting Guidelines

Many proposals have specific instructions for page formatting and font size. Oftentimes people will type their proposals and go back later to format the document. Make sure that you check to make sure that the entire document is formatted correctly. For instance, in Microsoft Word there is often a choice to change the formatting for a particular section or the whole document. Double check to make sure that your entire document is the correct font type and size if specified.

Mistake #8 – All Required Attachments and Information Not Included

If you do not include all of the required attachments and information, your proposal can be rejected and deemed incomplete. Make yourself a checklist of all attachments and documents required, and review this list before submission. If you are instructed to include a particular document "if applicable", make sure that you list the document and state that it is not applicable to your situation.

Some required documentation, such as proof of non-profit status, may take a while to get if you do not already have a copy. Make sure you order documents that you need from a third-party early enough that you can make your submission by the deadline. Remember, it can take several months to receive documents from government agencies. You should plan for this ahead of time.

Mistake #9 – Organization Has Not Been Formally Incorporated

Most proposals require that the applicant organization be a formally incorporated organization. Make sure that you have submitted the proper paperwork to your state's Secretary of State and have received notification back about your incorporation. If you have not formally incorporated, seek the advice of an attorney concerning which type of business structure best fits your organization.

Most states require some type of annual report to be filed every one or two years. Make sure that you have filed all of the necessary paperwork and that your organization is in good standing with your state and local government.

Mistake #10 – Legal Name Does Not Match DUN Number Registration

The Data Universal Numbering System or D-U-N-S® number is a unique nine-digit number that identifies business entities on a location-specific basis. This system is copyrighted by Dun & Bradstreet (D&B). A D-U-N-S® number remains with the company location to which it has been assigned even if it closes or goes out-of-business. The D-U-N-S® number was adopted as the standard business identifier for federal electronic commerce in October 1994. In April 1998 the D-U-N-S® number was incorporated into the Federal Acquisition Regulation (FAR) as the Federal Government's contractor identification code for all procurement-related activities, including grants.

In order to apply for any type of government grant, your organization must have a D-U-N-S® number. Registration is free. You can register here at http://fedgov.dnb.com/webform. Although it only takes a few days to receive your number, do not wait until the last minute to apply.

Make sure that the name on your D-U-N-S® registration matches the legal name of your organization. Remember, D-U-N-S® numbers are location specific. If your organization moves, you need a new number. Make sure the address associated with D-U-N-S® is the same address on your grant application.

Mistake #11 – Organization Does Not Have or Did Not Include EIN

An Employer Identification Number (EIN), also known as a Federal Tax Identification Number, is used to identify a business entity with the Internal Revenue Service. Most businesses and organizations, including non-profits will need an EIN at some point. You may apply online at http://www.irs.gov/Businesses/Small-Businesses-&-Self-Employed/Apply-for-an-Employer-Identification-Number-(EIN)-Online. This is a free service offered by the Internal Revenue Service.

Make sure that you have included your EIN in your grant proposal, if required. Many times, the person preparing the grant proposal may not know the organization's EIN and will leave it blank with the intentions of coming back to it. Make sure you go back and fill it in before you submit your proposal. If it is required and you fail to include it, your proposal can be considered incomplete.

Mistake #12 – Did Not Include Congressional District (if applicable)

Many government grants require that you include the congressional district your organization is located in. As most people do not know, off of the top of their heads, the exact district number, this item is often left blank with the idea that the grant writer will come back to it. Make sure that you actually do go back and fill out the required information. You can find out your congressional district online here: http://www.govtrack.us/congress/members.

Mistake #13 – Did Not Include Proof of IRS Tax Exempt Status (if applicable)

Many government and private grants require that your organization obtain official Internal Revenue Service (IRS) Tax Exemption. The most popular one is 501(c)(3) status, but there are others.

Do not confuse this tax exempt status with the tax exempt status offered by your local state which allows you tax exemptions on the purchases you make. The IRS tax exempt status is a rather complex document that must be submitted to the IRS with a user fee ranging from $300 to $750. Once submitted, it can take several months to receive a response.

There are some organizations which are exempt under the IRS statues that are not required to file for an official exemption. For instance, churches are generally considered 501(c)(3) exempt, even if they have not applied for the exemption. Of course, the IRS encourages these organizations to apply, anyway, so their donors are assured that they meet the requirement. If you are a church organization that decides not to apply, make sure that you state in your grant proposal that you are not required to apply. You may also want to include the exact language from the IRS that states this. But be advised, a grantor may require that you have an official IRS determination in order to apply for their grant.

Mistake #14 – Project Title Missing or Vague

Make sure that you include the title of your project. Your title should be clear, precise and not misleading. Try to include keywords that convey the essence of your project. The title is the reviewer's first impression of a grant application. "Project titles should be clever but not cutesy," say New and Quick in their book, *GrantSeeker's Toolkit: A Comprehensive Guide to Finding Funding*. Do your homework. Find out what program areas are popular and in line with funding priorities of the grantor's organization.

Mistake #15 – Abstract is Not Included or Poorly Written

The abstract should be clear, succinct, and well written. It should tell the reviewer what the project is about, who it will serve, the expected outcomes and why it is needed. This is your chance to make an initial impression on the reviewer and convince them that your proposal is worth reading further. Errors here, such as typos or wrong word choices, can be detrimental in this section. Make sure that you proofread this section several times to make sure it clearly represents your project and your organization.

Since the abstract is a summary of your proposal, it may be beneficial to write it last. Many people will write the abstract first because it is located first in the overall document. They will write the abstract based on what they are planning on writing in the other sections. However, as they get to the other sections, they may change direction in terms of materials they present. They then must go back and re-write the abstract in order to now fit the proposal. This may not always occur. As a result, the abstract ends up not quite fitting in proposal.

Mistake #16 – The Problem Addressed in the Proposal is Not Significant

Make sure you can support the importance of the problem you would like to address. Your program may address something that you are extremely passionate about, but it may not be significant especially when compared to other social problems. If your project falls into this category, it will be up to you to supply the data to support the significance of the problem you want to address.

Try to relate your issue to some of the larger social issues of the day. For instance, you may have a passion for exposing young people to art or music. While that is a very worthy cause, it may not be seen as important as addressing violence or drug use among youth. Find data that supports how young people that are exposed to music are less likely to be involved in violence and drug use. Go on further to suggest how involvement in music and arts can lead to improved reading and math scores, which leads to higher graduation rates and so on. However, you must paint the picture (no pun intended).

Mistake #17 – Proposal Does Not Include Enough Documentation about the Problem

Even if your proposal is addressing a high profile problem area, you must still include sufficient documentation about the problem. Make sure that you include statistics and case studies to sufficiently document the issue that you are addressing. You cannot rely on the notion that "everyone knows that violence among young people is an issue" as an excuse not to do the work. Remember, your proposal is not to just convince the reviewer that your issue is important. You are more importantly trying to convince the reviewer that you are well versed on the issue and that your organization has the best answer on how to address the issue.

Mistake #18 – Proposal Does Not Specifically State How the Money will be Used

Your proposal should clearly state how you plan to use the money you are requesting. Avoid general terms such as "operating expenses", "overhead" or "equipment purchases." Thoroughly detail the amount you are requesting and exactly what you plan to purchase. Also, make sure that your request meets the grant guidelines. For instance, some grants will state that the money cannot be used for salaries. Read the guidelines carefully.

Mistake #19 — Proposal Does Not Demonstrate Creativity or Innovation

Most grant proposals are based in great ideas. Most grant reviewers are familiar with the typical "great ideas" that are included in your proposal. However, your proposal must stand out from the rest. Your proposal must demonstrate creativity and innovation. This does not necessary mean that you must re-invent the wheel. However, your proposal must convince the reviewer that your organization is able to meet the grant objectives better than any of the other organizations that have submitted proposals.

Mistake #20 — Literature Review Does Not Include Relevant Research

Make sure your proposal includes relevant research regarding your project. Of course it is important for children to improve their reading skills. However, you must do a thorough literature review and include statistics on why this is so. For instance, if your project included a literacy program for middle school children, you should include research data and statistics on the current reading scores of the children in your program and the consequences of those scores not improving.

When citing literature research, make sure to include the title of the report, the organization that issued the report and the year, if possible.

Below is an example of such research included in a grant proposal for an after/out of school program.

> *The need for out-of-school programs for children has been documented in numerous studies over the last decade. The Education Commission of*

the States lists the following facts on their website regarding extended day programs.

- *Both parents had jobs in 60.7% of two-parent families in 2003 (U.S. Bureau of Labor Statistics, Employment Characteristics of Families Summary, April 2003)*

- *In 2003, the mother was employed in 71.9% of single parent families maintained by women, while the father was employed in 83.3% of single parent families maintained by men. (U.S. Bureau of Labor Statistics, Employment Characteristics of Families Summary, April 2003)*

- *After the school day ends, 14.3 million K-12 students take care of themselves, including almost 4 million students between grades 6 and 8. (After school Alliance, America After 3PM, 2004)*

- *Statistics show that most juvenile crime takes place between the hours of 2PM and 8PM, and that children also are at much greater risk of being the victims of crime during the hours after school. (U.S. Department of Education, After-School Programs, September 2000)*

Mistake #21 – Needs Assessment Does Not Clearly Articulate the Project Audience and Its Needs

Make sure that your proposal clearly articulates who will benefit from your program. You must include who your target market or audience is. Although it can be tempting to believe that "everyone" needs and will benefit from your program, you must be specific as to whom you are targeting. Yes, everyone could use a hot meal on a cold, winter day, but your target may be homeless people in a particular neighborhood. Make sure you clearly state that.

You must also establish that your target audience "needs" your service. Why can't your audience afford to buy their own meal? Why can't they cook for themselves? Make sure you clearly explain why your audience needs your program.

Mistake #22 – Does Not Provide Evidence That Project Activities and Goals Directly Address the Needs of the Identified Audience

Your proposal must clearly show how the project activities and goals directly address the needs of your identified audience. Although you may think that it is obvious, you should spell it out for the reviewer. Many times we become so involved in the work we are doing, we think that everyone sees our project the way we do. The connections that are obvious to us may not be obvious to others.

For instance, suppose you have an afterschool literacy center that you are seeking funds for. You have identified a funder and you want to apply for a grant to purchase kitchen equipment so that you can serve nutritious snacks. Your proposal should not only address the literacy needs of your audience, but it should also address the nutritional needs as well. Although it may be obvious that young people are hungry after school, you should include why it is important for you to feed them. In your proposal you state that for many of the children in your program, four hours will have passed since their last meal. You could cite the importance between nutritious snacks and concentration in children. Make sure that you make a connection between what you are asking for and the needs of your identified audience.

Mistake #23 – Does Not Clearly State Project Goals and Objectives

Make sure that your proposal clearly states the project's goals and objectives. Avoid unspecific, immeasurable objectives such as "we want to make the world a better place" or "we want to feed the hungry". Be specific in whom you want to help and what you want to help them with. Your goal should also include how you will know when they have been helped.

In his article, "Grant Writing Tip - How to Write SMART Objectives", Stephen Price explains that successful grant proposals include SMART objectives: Specific, Measurable, Attainable, Relevant, and Time Bound. This is similar to the SMART goals discussed in Paul J. Meyer's book, "Attitude Is Everything".

Specific

Goals must be specific. Make sure you answer the following questions when preparing your goals.

- Who is involved?
- What do we want to accomplish?
- Where will we accomplish it?
- When will it happen?
- Why do we need to reach this goal?

Measurable

Goals must be measurable. If your objective is to improve literacy, you need to explain how that will be measured. Will you use test scores or student progress reports? How much improvement are you looking for?

Attainable

Goals must be realistic. Although it would be wonderful to wipe out homelessness in your community, you probably will not be able to do that with a $10,000 grant. It may be more realistic to state that your organization's goal is to provide housing and job placement for 10 homeless individuals during the first year. Once you have reached that goal, you place yourself in a better position to receive funding to expand your program.

Relevant

Goals must relate to the measurable needs of the population that you serve and they must directly relate to your proposal. If you are proposing a literacy center, do not add goals that relate to health issues and hunger. Make sure your proposal stays focused on the priorities stated in your proposal.

Time-Bound

Make sure your proposal describes when your goals will be met. Deadlines provide for accountability.

Mistake #24 – Does Not Clearly State the Design, Integration, and Implementation of an Evaluation Method that will Measure Project Results

As mentioned before, it is important that your goals and objectives are measurable. Your proposal must clearly explain the evaluation method that you will use to accomplish this. This can be tricky because you do not want to include an exhaustive thesis on statistics and evaluation methods. However, you must include enough information to demonstrate that you know what you are talking about. For instance, if you are using a survey to measure project results, clearly explain the types of questions that are to be included. Also explain how the participant will receive the survey and how the results will be tabulated. If there are standard protocols that will be used, make sure to name them. Do your research.

Mistake #25 – Does Not Include Information About the Roles and Commitments of Partnering Organizations, if applicable

If your proposal includes partnering organizations, make sure you clearly define the roles and commitments of that organization. Refer to any documentation you have received from the organization. Of course, make sure you have spoken with the organization ahead of time and that they are willing operate in the role you have specified in your proposal. For instance, if want to use the pool at the local YMCA for your after-school program, make sure that you have those discussions with them BEFORE you list them in your proposal as a partner. Just because the YMCA has a pool it does not mean that they will allow your organization to use it, particularly if they have a similar program utilizing that space.

Mistake #26 – Does Not Identify Key Project Staff, Their Duties, and Their Qualifications for Successfully Completing Their Project Tasks

Your proposal should clearly identify key project staff, their duties, and their qualifications for successfully completing their project tasks. Make sure to include the person's name, not just their title. Many proposals request that you include a resume for each of the key staff members. Make sure the resume has been updated and includes the person's current role and responsibilities.

Make sure to highlight each staff member's qualifications as it relates to the project proposal. It is easy to do this if the person's education or work experience relates directly to the task. For instance, if the project requires someone to do bookkeeping and prepare monthly reports, you can state that Jane Doe, who has an accounting degree or who has worked as a bookkeeper for that last 15 years, will be responsible for this task without the need for a lot of additional explanation. However, if Jane Doe has no formal education or work experience in bookkeeping but has done it on a volunteer based for the last 10 years, this may need some further explanation. If your key staff person does not have formal training in the role they are fulfilling in your project, you may need to relate some of their past experience and training to the task at hand. For instance in the example given here, you may want to explain that Jane Doe has prepared financial reports for her block club for the last 15 years.

Mistake #27 — Does Not Identify Consultants and Service Providers Involved in Project Activities, the Process for Selecting Them, and How They Will Work With Project Staff

Your proposal should clearly identify any consultants and service providers involved in project activities, the process for selecting them, and how they will work with project staff. Will you use a bid process to select consultants or are you using consultants that you have worked with in the past? Make sure you carefully read the proposal criteria to see if there are any specific requirements for selecting service providers. Some Request for Proposals (RFP's) will require a specific bidding process.

Make sure you clearly state how these consultants and service providers will work with your project staff. Will they work in your facility or at another location? Will they come into contact with the people you serve? This is particularly important if you work with children. Many state and federal laws require that each person coming in contact with children in your facility meet the same requirements (i.e., drug screening and background checks) as your staff.

Mistake #28 — Does Not Include a Timeline for Specific Activities

Your proposal should clearly identify a timeline for the completion of specific activities associated with your project. This helps the reviewer understand your project better. Include milestones such as equipment purchases, training and important meetings. Also include monitoring milestones such as client assessments and customer feedback surveys.

Mistake #29 – Does Not Describe the Facilities, Equipment, and Supplies Necessary to Support the Project

Your proposal should describe facilities, equipment, and supplies necessary to support the project. Remember, the reviewer has probably never seen your facility. Make sure you paint a picture with your words that helps the reviewer visualize your facility. However, don't go overboard. It is not a novel. While you may describe the number of rooms and how these rooms will be used for the purpose of your project, the reviewer does not need to know the color of the floor.

Make sure you list the equipment and supplies that you need for your project. Clearly describe any equipment that may not be familiar to the reviewer. For instance, you can list that you need a photocopy machine without adding any additional description. However, if you also listed that you needed a gait trainer, you should probably add that this is a wheeled device that assists people who are unable to walk learn to walk safely.

Mistake #30 – Does Not Identify Source(s) of Matching Funds and/or In-kind Contributions (if applicable)

Make sure your proposal identifies the source of any matching funds or in-kind contributions if required by the RFP. Make sure you are specific in your description. For instance, don't state that a "local contractor" will provide an in-kind donation. List the contractor's name and general description of the type of work he/has has agreed to do.

Mistake #31 – Does Not Identify Source(s) and Use of Revenues That Will be Derived From the Project, if applicable

If your project generates revenue, make sure that you identify the source and the use for the revenue generated. Be sure to include it in your budget. Remember, non-profit does not mean that the organization does not make money. Non-profit means that the money made is put back into the organization and not paid out to stockholders. Organizations that consistently operate in the red or at the breakeven point are not sustainable over the long term.

Mistake #32 – Does Not Reflect Evidence of Sound Financial Management Coupled with an Appropriate and Cost-efficient Budget

Your project must demonstrate sound financial management. Your organization should have a bank account that is used solely for the operation of the organization. Personal transactions should not occur. Make sure you have a system for reimbursing personnel that spend their own money for items that are not considered a donation. If you have a petty cash system, make sure that you document, with receipts, any disbursements.

Sound financial management has at its core an appropriate and cost-efficient budget for the organization. This is not just the budget you put together for the project at hand. You should have a process in place for developing the budget for your organization. Your financial management should also include the development of financial reports that are reviewed on a regular basis. It is nice to have a budget, but it is useless if you are not checking it see if you are staying on track.

Mistake #33 – Does Not Reflect Evidence That All Partners are Active Contributors to the Partnership Activities (if applicable)

You should list people or organizations as partners only if they are active contributors to the project or organization. Don't list names just to list names or as a way of "name dropping". Also, make sure that the people or organizations that you list as partners know that you plan to list them in your proposal. It would be embarrassing if one of your partners were contacted and they indicated that they were not familiar with you or your project.

Mistake #34 – Evidence That the Project's Benefits Can be Sustained Beyond the Grant Period

Your proposal must demonstrate that the project's benefits can be sustained beyond the grant period. Funders want to know that their money is going to make a difference for years to come. You must show how you will continue to raise money for your project. This may include, but is not limited to fundraising, other grant monies, endowments and revenues generated.

Mistake #35 – Proposal Includes Not Enough Detail or Too Much Detail

Your proposal must include enough detail in order to demonstrate to the reviewer that you should be awarded the grant. However, you must be careful not to provide too much detail that you are wasting their time. It is a delicate balance. Make sure you provide answers that are thorough and precise. Also, pay particular attention to any word or character limitations for the proposal. If using an electronic system for grant submission, make sure to type your answers in a word processing program first so that you can check for errors. Most word processing programs will also tell you the word or character count for your text.

Mistake #36 – Proposal is Not Drawing a Clear Link Between Need, Plan, and Budget

Your proposal must draw a clear link between need, plan, and budget. Make sure you clearly explain the need that your proposal addresses. Many proposals state the "big picture" without clearly specifying which part of that picture that proposal will address. Once the specific need is clarified, make sure the plan does in fact address that specific need. For instance, the purpose of your literacy program may be to raise the reading level for minority students. Along with this "big picture" description, make sure you specify what your organization will do to help. Your program may be designed to help 100 minority students in a specific geography location. Make sure that is clear.

Also, make sure that your budget corresponds to your plan. If you are helping 100 students this year, that is what your budget should reflect. If you plan to expand your program over the next several years, make sure your budget reflects this expansion.

Mistake #37 – Proposal Sloppy and Difficult to Read

It is very important that your proposal is presented in a neat and professional manner. Make sure that your proposal is not sloppy. The pages should be neat and without wrinkles. Makes sure the proposal is printed properly and that there are no ink marks or partially printed pages.

Make sure that your proposal is not difficult to read. If the RFP does not specify exact font or page layout, use generally acceptable settings. For instance, a font size of 10-12 is generally acceptable for most proposals. Use black ink unless otherwise specified. Avoid fancy or hard to read font types. Remember, your proposal is being reviewed by people who are reading a number of good proposals on the same subject. Sloppy or difficult to read proposals are more likely to be eliminated.

Mistake #38 – Proposal Filled with Jargon

Do not use unnecessary jargon or acronyms. The proposal narrative should not be full of buzzwords and clichés, with little or no substance. Reviewers will see right through this. Make sure you use words carefully. Explain your subject matter thoroughly. Don't use certain words just to show off.

Mistake #39 – Organization Does Not Document Success with Other Grants/Projects

If your organization has successfully managed other grants, regardless of the size, make sure to include it in your narrative. If you are a new organization without a track record concerning grant management, include successful project management instead. Make sure to highlight any past grant management success that your staff or board members have had, even if it was with a different organization. You may have to be creative in this section but make sure that you are honest.

Mistake #40 – Organization Does Not Demonstrate Financial Stability

Make sure that your proposal demonstrates the financial stability of your organization. If your organization has operated in the red for the last several years, it may be difficult to convince the grantor that your organization will be around to carry out its mission. Grantors may be hesitant to fund your project if it appears that your organization is hemorrhaging and that those funds may be diverted and used to pay other expenses that your organization is facing.

Mistake #41 – The Project Doesn't Match the Funder's Objectives or Areas of Interest

You may have a wonderful proposal but if it does not match the funder's objective or area of interest, it may not go far. Make sure you research the funder carefully so that your submission is appropriate. You don't want to waste the funding organization's time submitting a proposal that is not appropriate. If you really want to work with that particular funding organization, consider changing your program to meet their criteria as long as it is consistent with the overall goals of your organization.

Mistake #42 – Budget is Incomplete

Make sure the budget information that you submit is complete. If the RFP has a budget form to complete, make sure that you include all appropriate entries. If there is no standard form available, make sure you include the following information:

- Income or Resources
- Personnel
- Fringe Benefits

- Travel
- Equipment
- Supplies
- Construction

Mistake #43 – Budget Contains Math Errors

Make sure you check and re-check your budget for math errors. If you are using a spreadsheet double check the formulas. It is a good idea to have someone else check the math before submitting. Although this is a very easy mistake to make, it can be very embarrassing and cause your proposal to be rejected.

Mistake #44 – Projected Income/Resources Do Not Make Sense

Make sure the projected income or program resources make sense. If your fundraising efforts in the past year has brought in $10,000, it does not make sense to project $50,000 for the upcoming year unless you can justify what you are doing differently that will result in a 500% increase in giving.

Mistake #45 – Projected Expenses Do Not Make Sense

Likewise, make sure the projected expenses make sense. Obviously expenses that are too large will raise a red flag. If the entire budget for the program is $150,000 and the Program Director's salary is $100,000, something appears to be wrong. However, expenses that are too small will also raise suspicion. For instance, renting a 5,000 square foot facility for $100 per month does not seem reasonable. The bottom line is the makes sure that your budget makes sense and does not appear as if you haphazardly threw numbers together.

Mistake #46 – Budget Narrative Does Not Justify Amounts

In the budget narrative, make sure that you describe how the budget is related to the proposed activities. Unless otherwise stated, you should include a separate statement for each project year. Every expense identified should appear in the narrative. Make sure you justify the reason for any expense that is not obvious. Also, include any assumptions used to calculate your numbers.

Mistake #47 – Budget Numbers Do Not Match Narrative and/or Summary

After you have worked and re-worked your budget and budget narrative, make sure that they match. It is common to make changes to the budget and/or narrative as you review your proposal. Sometimes, these changes are not reflected throughout your proposal.

Mistake #48 – Required financial records are not included

Make sure you submit all required financial records. They should be clearly labeled and placed in the appendix or wherever it is indicated. If you are required to submit bank statements, make sure you submit copies that are clear and easy to read. If audited financial statements are required, make sure to include the appropriate statements from your accountant.

Mistake #49 – Company Balance Sheet is Incorrect or Out of Balance

Make sure that the company's balance sheet is correct and reflects the appropriate balance. The balance sheet must follow the following formula:

Assets = Liabilities + Equity

Again, make sure you check the math.

Mistake #50 – Company Previous Profit/Loss Statements are Incorrect

Make sure that the company's Profit/Loss statements are correct. Check the math and make sure that numbers correspond with bank statements and other financial documents. For instance, if you stated that your organization received $200,000 last year but your bank statements only reflect $125,000 in deposits, you need to address the discrepancy.

References

http://blog.elpomar.org/?p=186

http://blogs.christianpost.com/pastor/the-deadliest-grant-writing-mistakes-made-by-christian-ministries-and-churches-2670/

http://nonprofit.about.com/od/foundationfundinggrants/tp/proposalmistakes.htm

http://professionalwritingservices.net/grantwritingmistakes.html

http://veronicarobbins.hubpages.com/hub/novice-grant-writer-mistakes

http://www.chicagomanualofstyle.org/home.html

http://www.content-professionals.com/Grant-Writing-Tips.php

http://www.grantstation.com/Public/tracks_to_success/Mistakes/1.asp

http://www.grantstation.com/Public/tracks_to_success/Mistakes/2.asp

http://www.grantstation.com/Public/tracks_to_success/Mistakes/3.asp

http://www.hort.purdue.edu/rhodcv/hort652n/ho00007.htm

http://www.idiotsguides.com/static/quickguides/reference/the-10-most-common-grant-writing-mistakes.html

http://www.nimh.nih.gov/funding/grant-writing-and-application-process/common-mistakes-in-writing-applications.shtml

http://www.pamelasgrantwritingblog.com/461/8-biggest-grant-proposal-mistakes/

http://www.quickanddirtytips.com/grammar-girl

Other Books by Heart Thoughts Publishing

Intensive Faith Therapy – Vanessa Collins

The Promises of Jesus – Vanessa Collins

The Promises of God – Vanessa Collins

Transcending Greatness – Lawrence Perkins

Lil Fella's Big Dream – Lawrence Perkins

One Way – Dorsey Howard

Breakfast with God – Paul Jakes

The Start of a Healing Conversation – Edgar Gosa

Visit us at **www.HeartThoughtsPublishing.com**

Or email us at

Info@HeartThoughtsPublishing.com

www.ingramcontent.com/pod-product-compliance
Lightning Source LLC
Chambersburg PA
CBHW071827170526
45167CB00003B/1450